World Book, Inc.
180 North LaSalle Street
Suite 900
Chicago, Illinois 60601
USA

For information about other "True or False?" titles, as
well as other World Book print and digital publications,
please go to www.worldbook.com.

For information about other World Book publications,
call 1-800-WORLDBK (967-5325).

For information about sales to schools and libraries,
call 1-800-975-3250 (United States) or 1-800-837-5365
(Canada).

Library of Congress Cataloging-in-Publication Data for
this volume has been applied for.

True or False?
ISBN: 978-0-7166-3725-7 (set, hc.)

The Solar System
ISBN: 978-0-7166-3733-2 (hc.)

Also available as:
ISBN: 978-0-7166-3743-1 (e-book)

Printed in China by Shenzhen Wing King Tong Paper
Products Co., Ltd., Shenzhen, Guangdong
1st printing July 2018

Staff

A light-year is an amount of time.

FALSE!

A light-year is the distance light travels in a year. It's about 5.88 trillion miles (9.46 trillion kilometers)! Astronomers *(uh STRON uh muhrz)* are scientists who study space and its moons, planets, and stars. They measure the huge distances between things in space in light-years.

The sun is white.

TRUE!

The sun is a star. It gives off white light. The atmosphere, or the layer of air around Earth, makes the sun appear orange and yellow to our eyes. The sun looks like a giant ball of fire in the sky! It provides light, heat, and other energy to Earth.

18

19

TRUE OR FALSE?

More than one million Earths could fit inside the sun.

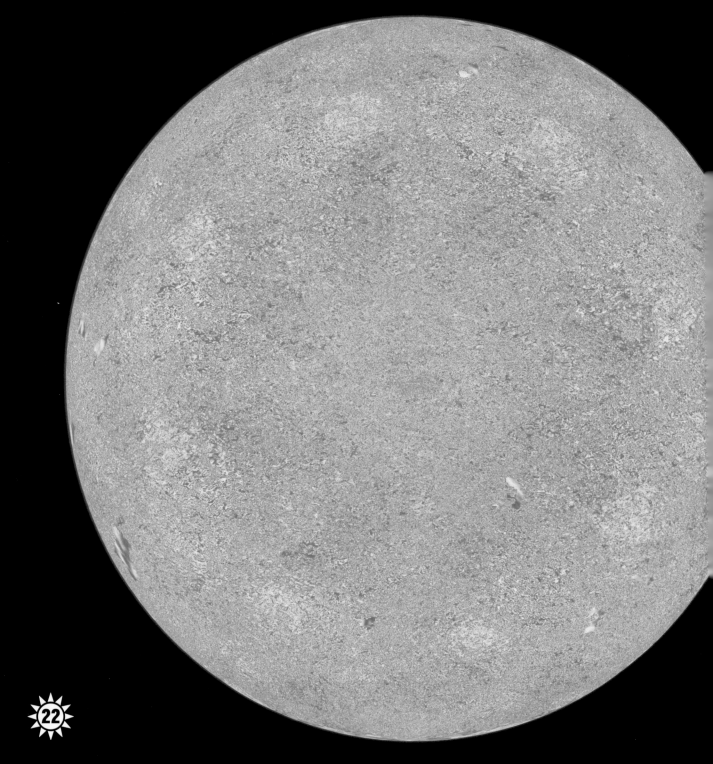

Earth

The sun is the biggest thing in our solar system. It is so big that it could hold about 1,300,000 Earths!

The moon only comes out at night.

The moon is always traveling around Earth. We see the moon easily at night because the sky is dark and the sun lights up the moon. Often, we can see the moon during the daytime, too!

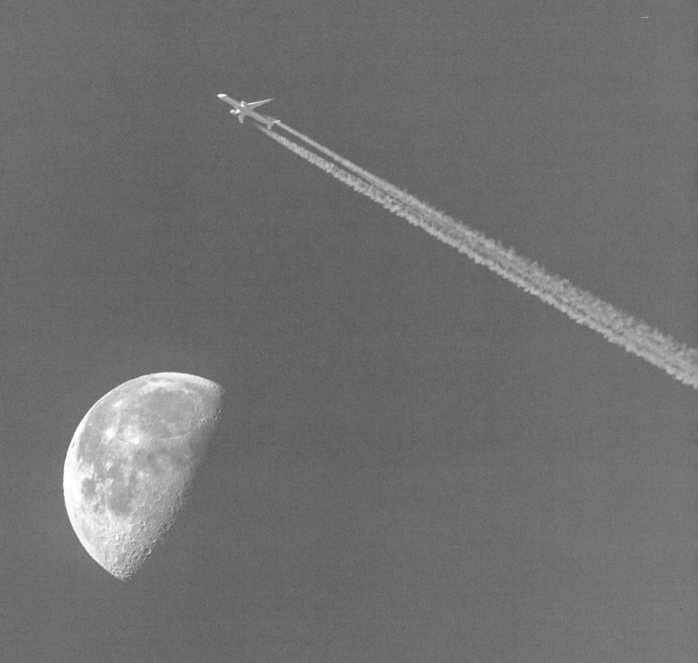

Asteroids and comets are all made of the same stuff.

Asteroids are large rocky or metallic objects. They orbit the sun like planets do, but they are much smaller. Comets are large balls of ice and dust—like dirty snowballs moving through space!

Venus and Earth are twins.

But they are not identical. Venus and Earth are nicknamed "twin planets" because they are about the same size, and no other planet is nearer to Earth than Venus. Venus is a very different planet than Earth, though. The temperature on the surface of Venus is about 860 °F (460 °C). That's hotter than most ovens!

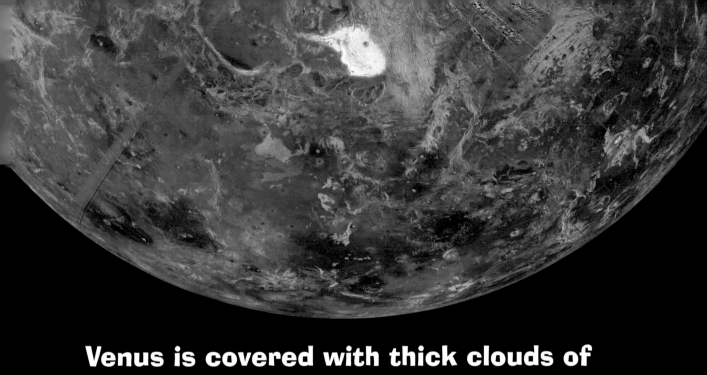

Venus is covered with thick clouds of deadly acid. Scientists do not think anything could live on Venus.

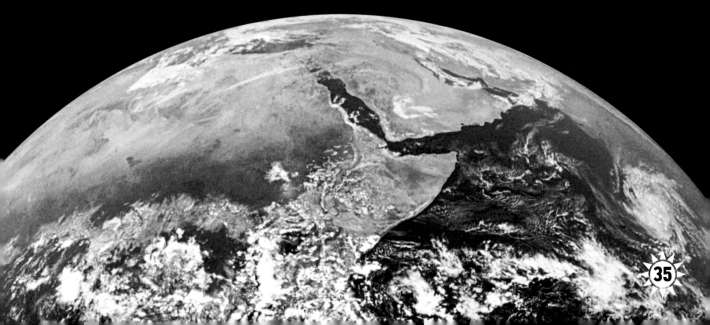

36

TRUE OR FALSE?

There is still gravity in space.
It's called "microgravity."

Astronauts float in space.
But it's not because there is
no gravity. The gravity just
works differently!

TRUE OR FALSE?

Mars, the Red Planet, is freezing cold.

41

42

It is usually around -80 °F (-62 °C) on the surface of Mars. That's way below freezing! The plants and animals that live on Earth could not survive on Mars. Mars is called the Red Planet because of its red soil, not because of its heat.

6'4"
6'2"
6'0"
5'10'
5'8"
5'6"
5'4"
5'2"
5'0"
4'10'
4'8"

44

Astronauts get taller in space.

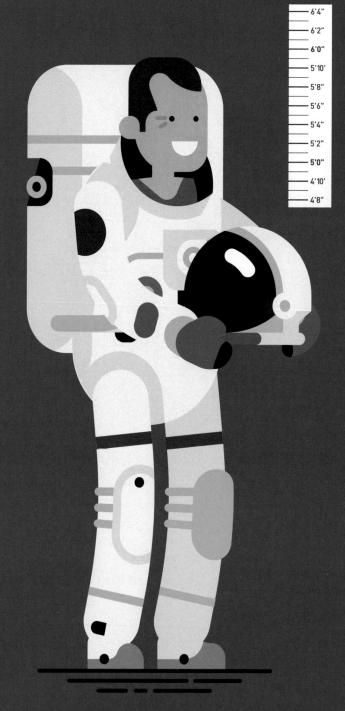

After about a year in space, NASA astronaut Scott Kelly was 2 inches taller than he had been before! In microgravity, an astronaut's spine expands. This makes him or her a little taller. When astronauts come back to Earth, though, they shrink back to their original height.

TRUE OR FALSE?

There are other stars
in our solar system.

49

FALSE!

The sun is the only star in our solar system. There are other stars outside our solar system. In the Milky Way galaxy alone, there are hundreds of billions of other stars! Other stars have planets that orbit them in their own solar systems. The next closest star is 4.3 light-years away from us.

The moon changes shape.

We see the moon change from a slim crescent shape to a full circle and back again. But the moon does not really change its size or shape. The amount of sunlight reflected by the moon toward Earth changes.

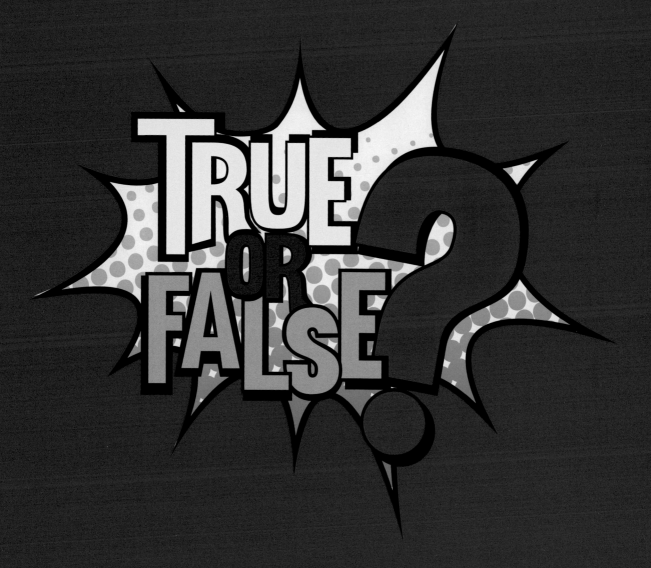

You can see other planets
without a telescope.

You can see Mercury, Venus, Mars, Jupiter, Saturn, and Uranus without a telescope.

Planets don't twinkle like stars. So, if you see something bright in the night sky that is shining with a solid light, you probably found a planet!

Earth is the center of our solar system.

Hundreds of years ago, people believed that everything orbited around Earth. We now know that the sun is the center of our solar system. Everything in our solar system orbits around the sun.

TRUE OR FALSE?

Shooting stars are not stars at all.

TRUE!

Shooting stars look like stars zooming across the night sky. But they are actually meteors!

These streaks of light are small bits of stuff that light up when they enter Earth's atmosphere. Air rubs against the hard stuff and heats it. This makes it glow and leave a shining trail. The brightest meteors are sometimes called fireballs.

TRUE OR FALSE?

The planets are all made of solid rock.

Some of the planets are mostly made of rock and metal. But Jupiter, Saturn, Uranus, and Neptune are made mostly of gas with a rocky center. They are called the gas giants. These gases can give them beautiful colors.

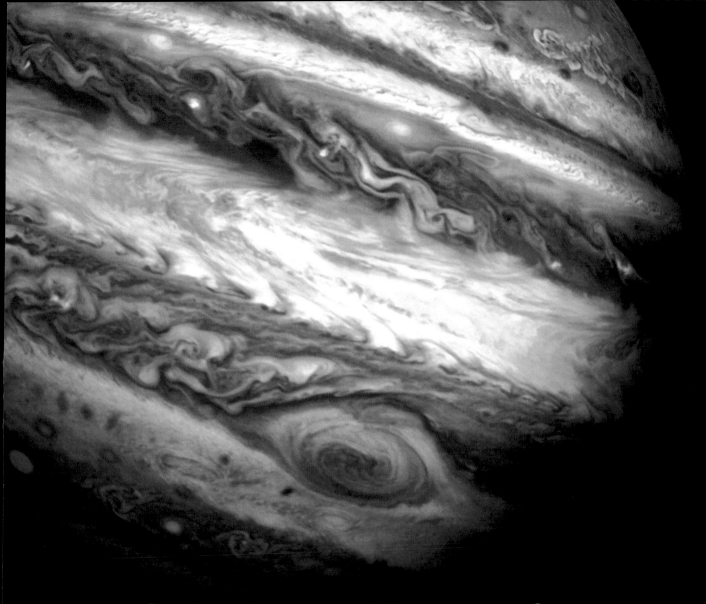

**Jupiter has a swirling spot of
gases that looks red. Scientists
call it the Great Red Spot.**

TRUE OR FALSE?

Some planets are decorated with rings.

TRUE!

The planets made of gas have rings. But they are not jewelry! Planets' rings are flat, disk-shaped areas. From far away, these rings may look solid. But they are made of floating bits of rock, dust, and ice.

The bits can be as tiny as a grain
of sand or as big as a house!

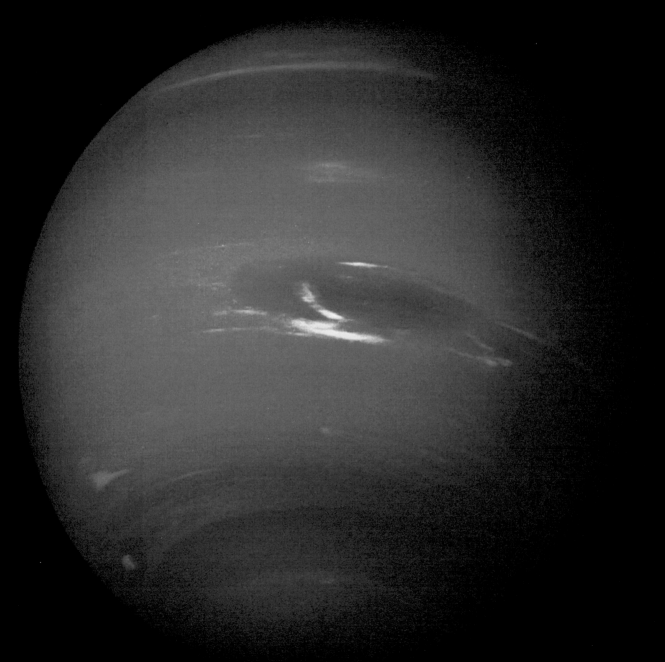

TRUE OR FALSE?

Neptune has a stripe around its center called the Main Belt.

The Main Belt is a place between Mars and Jupiter where there are tens of thousands of asteroids. Some people call this the asteroid belt.

Mars

Jupiter

The Main Belt

Pluto was once called a planet,
but now it is not.

Uranus

Neptune

Pluto

Mercury

Saturn

Sun

Venus

Jupiter

Mars

Earth

Moon

81

When Pluto was discovered in 1930, astronomers thought it was a planet. Now, Pluto is called a dwarf planet. A dwarf planet is an object orbiting the sun that is smaller than a planet and larger than a comet or meteor.

Dust devils are tiny storms on Mars that look like tornadoes.

86

TRUE!

Some of the most amazing weather occurs on Mars when dust blows in the wind. Small, swirling winds can lift dust off the surface for a while, making dust devils.

Scientists have learned everything about the solar system.

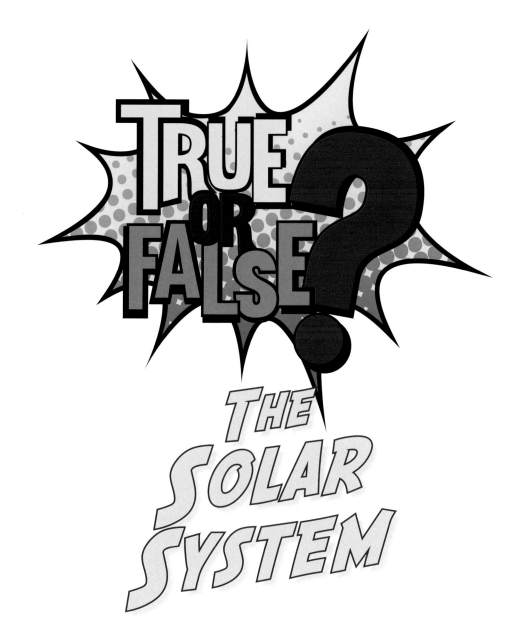

TRUE OR FALSE?

THE SOLAR SYSTEM

WORLD
BOOK

www.worldbook.com

TRUE OR FALSE?

Our solar system is about
5 billion years old.

4

The solar system is made up of the sun, Earth, and the other planets. It also includes such smaller objects as asteroids, meteoroids, and comets that orbit (travel around) the sun. The eight planets in our solar system are called Mercury, Venus, Earth, Mars, Jupiter, Saturn, Uranus, and Neptune.

Sun

Mercury

Venus

Earth

Mars

Jupiter

Saturn

Uranus

Neptune

7

There is only one moon.

Earth has only one moon. But some of the other planets have their own moons, too. Only Mercury and Venus do not have moons.

Jupiter has dozens of moons!

The solar system is a vast and wondrous place. Scientists have learned a lot, but there is much, much more to study and discover! You could be the next great astronomer or astronaut!

DID YOU KNOW...

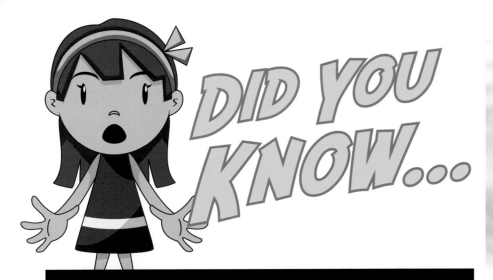

There are more stars in the universe than there are **grains of sand** on every beach on Earth!

For a long time, Earth was the only rocky planet known to have liquid water on its surface. Evidence now suggests that **Mars has water, too!**

Sunsets on Mars are **blue.**

The sun is **huge and heavy.**

It makes up 99.8 percent of the solar system's mass!

Scientists have sent spacecraft to

every planet in the solar system.

Pluto is a **dwarf planet.**
There are other dwarf planets in our solar system, too!

Pluto   Eris   Haumea   Makemake   Ceres

Our solar system is in the
Milky Way galaxy.

There's a candy bar named after it!

Index

Acknowledgments

Cover: ©Tatiana Apanasova, Shutterstock; © DRB Images/
        iStockphoto; © Ded Mazay, Shutterstock
5-31   © Shutterstock
33   NASA; © Anna Violet, Shutterstock
35   NASA
36-46   © Shutterstock
48-49   NASA/JPL-Caltech/UCLA
50-75   © Shutterstock
76   NASA/JPL
79-83   © Shutterstock
85   © Jordi Stock/iStockphoto
86   D. Mitriy/NASA/JPL (licensed under CC BY-SA 3.0)
88-93   © Shutterstock